Daily Life in ANCIENT ROME

Don Nardo

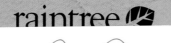

raintree

Raintree is an imprint of Capstone Global Library Limited, a company incorporated in England and Wales having its registered office at 7 Pilgrim Street, London, EC4V 6LB – Registered company number: 6695582

www.raintreepublishers.co.uk
myorders@raintreepublishers.co.uk

Edited by Clare Lewis
Designed by Philippa Jenkins
Original illustrations © Capstone Global Library Limited 2015
Illustrated by Roger@KJA-artists.com
Picture research by Jo Miller
Production by Helen McCreath
Originated by Capstone Global Library Ltd
Printed and bound in China

ISBN 978 1 406 28806 3 (hardback)
18 17 16 15 14
10 9 8 7 6 5 4 3 2 1

ISBN 978 1 406 28812 4 (paperback)
19 18 17 16 15
10 9 8 7 6 5 4 3 2 1

British Library Cataloguing in Publication Data
A full catalogue record for this book is available from the British Library.

Acknowledgements
We would like to thank the following for permission to reproduce photographs: Alamy: Heritage Image Partnership Ltd/Werner Forman Archive, 12, 35, Image Asset Management Ltd., 20, Lebrecht Music and Arts Photo Library, 28, Martin Shields, 19, North Wind Picture Archives, 30, 39; Corbis: Araldo de Luca, 14, 23, National Geographic Society/ Herbert M. Herget, 37, Vanni Archive, 31; Getty Images: Culture Club, 18, De Agostini /DEA Picture Library/A. Dagli Orti, 24, De Agostini/DEA Picture Library, 10, The Bridgeman Art Library/Herbert M. Herget, 8, 26; Mary Evans Picture Library: Illustrated London News Ltd, 29; Newscom: 20TH CENTURY FOX/Album, 32, Oronoz/Album, 34, Prisma/Olimpia Torres/Album, 16, Robert Harding/John Ross, 6, VWPics/Paulo Amorim, 40, World History Archive, 33; Shutterstock: irisphoto1, 22, John Copland, cover, Renata Sedmakova, 7, WitR, 5, worradirek, 41; UIG via Getty Images: LTL, 36 Design Elements: Nova Development Corporation, clip art (throughout), Shutterstock: imanolqs

We would like to thank Professor Ray Laurence for his help in the preparation of this book.

Every effort has been made to contact copyright holders of material reproduced in this book. Any omissions will be rectified in subsequent printings if notice is given to the publisher.

CONTENTS

Some words are shown in bold, **like this**. You can find out what they mean by looking in the glossary.

The ancient Romans were one of the most successful peoples in history. Their nation lasted from about 750 **BC** to **AD** 476 – more than 1,200 years! During those years, their armies conquered one country after another. At its height, in the 200s AD, the Roman Empire covered much of Europe. It also included Britain, North Africa and parts of the Middle East.

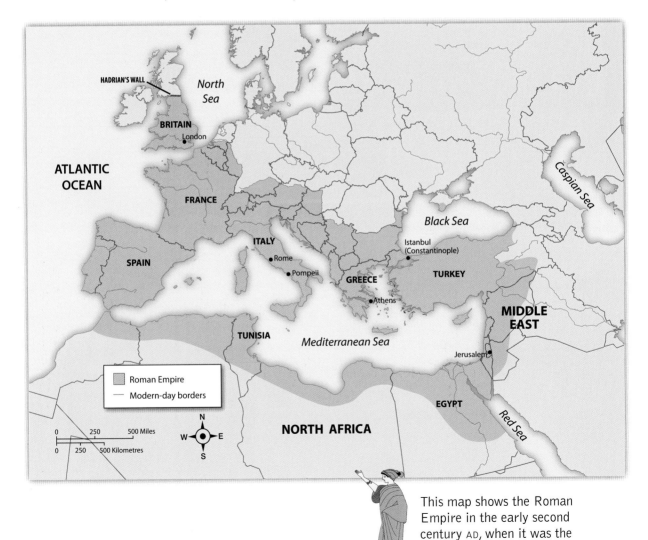

This map shows the Roman Empire in the early second century AD, when it was the largest it had ever been.

This stone arch was built to celebrate a military victory, and still survives today.

A talent for the practical

This remarkable achievement occurred for several reasons. One was that the Romans had an amazing talent for solving practical problems. Also, they regularly applied that ability to building things. Roman painters, sculptors, and musicians created some wonderful works. But the true Roman artist was an **engineer**, or master builder. Rome's world empire was created as much by its engineers as by its armies.

The Romans were also great borrowers. Often they chose the best ideas of other peoples and cleverly adapted them to their own needs. A good example was the *scutum*, the rectangular shield used by Rome's soldiers. The early Romans adapted it from a neighbouring Italian people, the Samnites. Rome also borrowed many religious and artistic ideas from the Greeks.

The Romans were determined to win and survive at all costs. The second-century BC Greek writer Polybius noticed this. He told of "how spirited and daring the Romans are when they are determined to do a thing".

Each new generation of Romans led their daily lives in a society that strongly emphasized being practical and determined. The result was that Romans, rich and poor, young and old, became flexible and strong as a people. So Rome's civilization was successful and long lasting.

From 30 BC to AD 476, Rome's lands were called the Roman Empire. The Empire was ruled by a long series of very powerful leaders, called emperors.

The Empire reached its height of power and influence in its first 200 years. In that time, most emperors were thoughtful and effective. Only a few, like the cruel, murderous Nero, were poor rulers. Most of Rome's residents led safe, happy lives.

The privileged few

Yet some people were happier, or at least more fortunate, than others. At the top of the social ladder was the emperor. And just below him were two groups of nobles.

THE FIRST EMPEROR

The first, most famous, and arguably greatest Roman emperor was Augustus. Born in 63 BC, when Rome was a **republic** run by elected leaders, he was known as Octavian. He rose to power during a period of bloody **civil wars**. In 30 BC, he emerged as both victor and sole commander of Rome's huge military. Seeing no other choice, the nobles accepted his authority and renamed him Augustus. Although he never called himself emperor, he was in fact the first of many.

Cicero was a powerful politician, writer and speaker.

The emperor and nobles made up only a tiny fraction of Rome's population. Yet they largely controlled society. They also led lives of luxury, with many servants. Partly, such high **social status** came from tradition. It had long been thought that nobles were better than commoners.

Tradition also claimed that men were cleverer than women. With some exceptions, therefore, Roman men controlled the lives of their wives, mothers and daughters.

Clients and patrons

Commoners, or plebs, made up the bulk of the Empire's population. They were mostly people of modest or poor means, such as farmers.

The commoners' low social status worked against them in several ways. The most visible one was a social system called **patronage**. In it, a commoner, the **client**, and a noble, the **patron**, had an arrangement. In theory, it was supposed to benefit both. But the wealthy and influential patron usually got more from the relationship. Some clients took part in the arrangement one or two days a week, while others did so almost every

People of all social classes mill about in Rome's port town of Ostia. A rich patron usually walked along with several of his clients.

HOW DO WE KNOW?

The decent patron

Some patrons treated their clients rudely. Such a person might keep them waiting for hours. Or he might demand much from them and give little in return. Such bad behaviour is known because the Roman noble and playwright Seneca the Younger wrote about it.

day.

Such a day began early in the morning with the *salutatio*, or "morning salute". The client washed and put on fresh clothes. He then walked to his patron's home. There, the client politely greeted the patron. The patron then explained the favours he wanted the client to perform that day. For example, the patron might take him and other clients along with him on social calls. This was because travelling with a group of loyal followers enhanced the patron's reputation. If he had to make a speech or appear in court, he would bring along as many clients as possible. They would frequently clap and cheer for him, making him look more impressive.

In return for such favours, the client might receive a bit of money. But a much better reward was an invitation to dine at the patron's house. Besides free food, the client got to socialize with people of a higher social status.

The size and quality of a Roman's house depended on its owner's income and social status. The emperors lived in huge palaces with many rooms and hundreds of servants. And the nobles had large, comfortable townhouses. They also had large country houses called **villas**.

This cut-away drawing shows a wealthy Roman home. The large area with the tiled floor and square-shaped pool is the atrium.

Homes of the rich and famous

These townhouses and villas were usually made of brick. Most often they were built around an inner courtyard that was open to the sky. Various rooms lined or led to the courtyard. The house's entrance hall, the **atrium**, was usually decorated with tiled flooring, statues and wall paintings. Also common in the atrium was a small **shrine** where family members prayed.

One or more corridors led from the atrium to the courtyard and other rooms. These included a kitchen, dining area, a few bedrooms and a study used mainly by the father. There were also some small servants' quarters and sometimes a bathroom. The bathroom frequently had stone channels that carried toilet waste to the city's **sewers**. Most bathrooms lacked baths because a majority of Romans preferred bathing in public bathhouses.

More often than not, townhouses and villas had pleasant gardens. This was because all Romans loved nature. When gardening, some Romans got the family slaves to help them, but others preferred to do it themselves.

HADRIAN'S VAST VILLA

Not surprisingly, the biggest and most luxurious Roman villa was built for an emperor. That ruler, Hadrian, reigned from AD 118 to 138. Located at Tivoli, then not far from Rome, it was not a single structure. It included Hadrian's vast living quarters, a bathhouse, two theatres and several gardens. Evidence shows that Hadrian himself designed some of the villa's luxuries.

Furniture

By modern standards, ancient Roman townhouses and villas did not have much furniture. Yet they had a stylish, elegant look. Because their owners were wealthy, the houses featured large-scale wall paintings. There were also statues and **mosaics**. The most common piece of furniture was a couch with a padded seat and soft pillows. Small round, three-legged tables frequently stood beside the couches and chairs. Beds had a wooden frame covered by a mattress of cloth stuffed with feathers or wool.

A surviving Roman couch with a padded seat sits in front of a faded but still visible wall painting.

GLASS AND WINDOWS

For many centuries, Roman windows had no transparent, or see-through, glass. People stretched sheepskin or oil cloth over them. Or they installed glass that was milky or blurry. Around AD 50, however, transparent glass became widely available. But it was expensive, so only the wealthy could afford it.

Less wealthy people owned many of the same items, except that they were rarely padded. The mattresses were more cheaply made and often lacked frames. Bedrooms in all but the very poorest homes also had one or more wooden chests for storage.

Lighting and heating

People of all social classes used candles and pottery or metal lamps. The lamps burned olive oil or other vegetable oils. Some lamps sat on tables, while others hung from ceilings.

When needed, heat came from a **hypocaust**. It was invented in about 100 BC by a merchant called Gaius Sergius Orata. Beneath a room to be heated was a brick-lined hollow space about 60 centimetres (2 feet) deep. It connected to a fire-burning furnace just outside the house. The heated air from the furnace drifted into the space, warming the floor. The most complex versions had similar spaces inside the walls. Hypocausts were expensive to install. So, with a few exceptions, they were found mainly in upper-class houses.

Lower-class homes

The homes of Roman commoners were modest compared to those of the wealthy. Farmers' huts were often pieced together with stones or mud-bricks and thatch (bundled tree branches). They had one or two small rooms with dirt floors. And there were few, if any, pieces of furniture. A central hearth provided heat and a place to cook. Family members got their water from the nearest stream or pond.

This is a model of the first three floors of a real apartment block that once stood at the foot of Rome's Capitoline Hill.

In contrast, poor people in Rome and other cities lived mainly in *insulae*. These inexpensive, crowded blocks of flats were made of concrete, bricks, wood and plaster. And they stood from three to six or more storeys high.

Typical flats had one or two tiny rooms. They had no running water, so people had to fill buckets at a nearby public fountain and carry them up several flights of stairs.

The poet Juvenal lived in such a flat in the Subura. It was the city of Rome's most heavily populated neighbourhood. Juvenal described it, saying it was a dangerous place to live. From time to time, some insulae collapsed, killing and injuring many. No one deserved to have "his house collapsing about his ears," he complained. The typical **tenement** "is poised like a house of cards [about] to collapse".

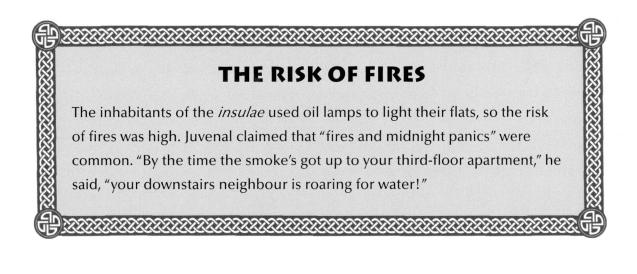

THE RISK OF FIRES

The inhabitants of the *insulae* used oil lamps to light their flats, so the risk of fires was high. Juvenal claimed that "fires and midnight panics" were common. "By the time the smoke's got up to your third-floor apartment," he said, "your downstairs neighbour is roaring for water!"

The ancient Romans ate many of the same foods that people eat today. However, the manner in which they cooked and ate them was different. Most cooking was done on open hearths lined with bricks or stone. Typically, a hearth was located in the kitchen. An iron grid mounted on top provided a surface for placing cooking pots.

This reconstruction shows how the kitchen in a Roman house would have looked.

Cooking in the city

Cooking on a hearth worked fine in ground-floor homes. The problem was that most city-dwellers lived higher up in the multi-storeyed *insulae*. Equipping all those flats with charcoal-burning hearths was too dangerous. It would have caused too many fires.

So the wealthy owners of the ground floors of city dwellings were the only people who could cook and eat in on a regular basis. And only they could throw dinner parties with home-cooked food. The far more common poorer people could have a cold breakfast at home. But for a hot meal, they had to go out to eat.

Common meals

Whether they ate in or out, most Romans ate a light breakfast of bread and sometimes cheese or fruit. Typical lunches included salad, bread and fruit.

Dinner, or *cena*, was the main meal. Common meats included lamb, poultry, fish and the Romans' favourite, pork. Also frequently eaten were stews that mixed meats with vegetables like carrots, onions and cabbage. Usual desserts included nuts, fruit, pudding, cake and other pastries.

COMMON DRINKS

Most Romans drank wine, which they mixed with water. Indeed, people saw drinking unmixed wine as very bad mannered. Adding honey to wine created another popular drink called mulsum. Some people in the Empire's northern provinces also drank beer.

This modern picture shows Romans feasting in the garden while musicians play.

Going out for dinner

Those city-living Romans without cooking facilities in their homes had several options. One was to buy items that would keep for a few days. Examples were bread, cheese and fruit. Cheese, fruit and other food items were sold in open-air marketplaces. Bread came from small bakeries, of which there were many in the average city.

POLITE DINING

At normal meals, most Romans sat upright on chairs, as people do today. At upscale dinner parties, however, diners rested on their sides on couches. The couches were assigned by the host. The higher one's social status, the closer the diner sat to the host.

After the food was served, the guests ate it with their fingers. However, there were exceptions for items like soup and pudding. Diners used spoons for those. Also, the guests usually brought their own napkins, which doubled as "doggy bags". A diner wrapped his leftovers in a napkin and took them home.

Hundreds of snack bars

Modern experts know a lot about Roman *thermopolii*. This is because the remains of more than 200 of them were unearthed at Pompeii. That small city, on Italy's western coast, was buried in ash during a volcanic eruption in AD 79.

Another alternative was to go out for a quick meal. Roman cities had many small snack bars (or cook shops) called *thermopolii*. Each had a wide bar or counter that was open to the pavement. The counter had a small metal grill for cooking meat, stew and soup. Like modern barbecues, the grill rested above a charcoal fire. There were also a number of pottery containers recessed into the counter. Some kept already cooked food warm. Others held uncooked items, such as raw vegetables, cheese, pastries and fruits.

Snack bars sold wine, as did taverns. The taverns served mostly the same foods that snack bars did, but were a bit larger. A tavern also had a few tables and chairs so that customers could sit and eat. Bigger still were formal restaurants. They had huge menus, along with one or more dining rooms with tables and chairs.

This Roman snack bar was discovered in Pompeii.

19

Roman family life was, like Roman society, male-dominated. Men usually made most of the important decisions for their wives and children. However, wives' position in the family, and women's rights in general, did improve over time.

This 19th century painting shows a Roman father and head of his household, on the right, along with members of his family.

Fathers and the family women

The father and husband in a Roman family was called the **paterfamilias**. The husband controlled all the family property. And only he could file for divorce. The wife's roles were to raise the children and manage the home.

But by the early years of the Empire, women could inherit and control their own property. They could also ask for divorce. In fact, divorces were very common and easy to obtain throughout the Empire period. Also, most wives now had a say in how the family's money was spent.

Arranging marriages

Wives almost certainly advised their husbands in arranging their children's marriages. Young men and women usually did not choose who they would marry on their own. Instead, the fathers of a boy and girl would agree that those young people should become engaged. Girls could be engaged at the age of seven and married at the age of twelve. However, most girls waited at least until their mid-teenage years to get married. The boy was typically a bit older when he got married – in his late teenage years or early twenties.

HOW DO WE KNOW?

Deeply in love

Many men deeply loved and respected their wives. This is known partly because the letters of a nobleman, Pliny the Younger, have survived. He addressed one to his wife, Calpurnia, when she was away. "You cannot believe how much I miss you," he wrote. "I love you so much [that] I stay awake most of the night thinking of you."

Having children

One of the central activities of Roman family life was having children. It was important to have children to inherit the family's property. Couples also had children at least partly to take care of them in their old age. People who were unable to have children often adopted.

TO KEEP OR REJECT A CHILD?

When a new baby arrived, a Roman father decided whether to keep or reject it. A common reason for rejection was deformity or some other handicap. In that case, the Romans left the infant outside to die. However, quite a few of these abandoned children were rescued by childless couples. This was the theme of a famous Roman myth. In the story, Rome's future founders, Romulus and Remus, were left to die. But a female wolf found and nursed them. Later, a shepherd and his wife raised the boys.

This sculpture shows a she-wolf caring for Rome's founders, Romulus and Remus.

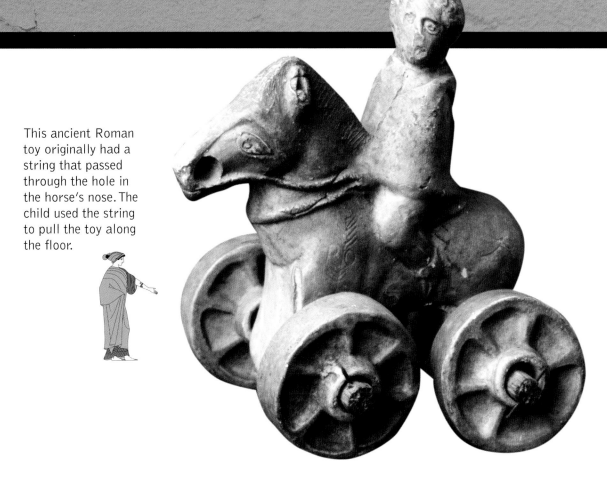

This ancient Roman toy originally had a string that passed through the hole in the horse's nose. The child used the string to pull the toy along the floor.

Roman children were almost always born at home. Most babies were delivered by a **midwife**, usually helped by the women of the household. Usually, a woman delivered her child sitting in an upright position in a special birthing chair. A ceremony to name the infant took place nine days later.

Playing with toys

As they grew older, children played with toys. Many toys were similar to modern ones. Girls had dolls, along with dollhouses, and boys had miniature wagons and chariots. Girls and boys enjoyed hoops, tops, seesaws, swings and marbles. Children also played with and took care of family pets. Just like today, many families had dogs and cats. It was also common to keep ducks, mice, snakes, pigeons and other birds.

Getting an education

During the early Empire, parents had to pay for their children to go to school, so only children from families that could afford it went to a primary school, or *ludus*. Both boys and girls attended from the age of seven. They learned basic reading and writing skills. But after three or four years, girls had to leave school to start preparing for marriage.

In this ancient Roman sculpture, a teacher holding a writing board is surrounded by his students.

Boys, meanwhile, continued on to secondary school. There, they studied history, geography, geometry, music and sometimes Greek. A few young men went on to learn **rhetoric** (public speaking) from private tutors. This skill was essential for men who wanted to enter one of Rome's two most celebrated professions – politics and law.

In contrast, most children from poor families never went to school. This is why many Romans were unable to read or write. Those young people usually began working at an early age. In the countryside, both boys and girls helped their parents by doing farm and household chores. In the cities, a boy started learning his father's trade or became an apprentice to another adult worker. A girl learned from her mother or other family women how to cook and make clothes.

WRITING MATERIALS

Paper was made from **papyrus**, a marsh plant that grew mainly in Egypt. People joined together separate sheets to make rolls about 9 metres (30 feet) long. Each roll was called a book. People wrote on papyrus with a pen made from a river reed or from bronze. They dipped the pen's tip into ink made from soot. Pupils or writers also used thin sheets of wood called leaf-tablets. People could write directly on the wood or cover it with wax and press a pointed object into the wax.

Rome had the largest number of slaves in human history. One third of the population of Italy was made up of slaves. These were non-citizens who had no personal freedom. The masters who owned them forced them to do various kinds of work. Most slaves' jobs were difficult, boring and sometimes dangerous. Household slaves cleaned, cooked, did repairs and ran errands. Farm slaves cleared land, planted crops and herded animals. And public slaves – those owned by the government – cleaned the streets, dug ditches, toiled in mines and helped government officials.

Slaves everywhere

During the early Empire, there were two main sources of slaves. One was "breeding" them by allowing existing slaves to have children. The other source was buying new slaves from slave markets.

Poorer homes had few or no slaves because they could not afford to feed and house them. In richer families, there were probably five to ten slaves. Very wealthy Roman homes had 50, 80 or even hundreds of slaves, depending on the owners' incomes. It was said that a rich man called Gaius Caelius Isidorus had 4,116 slaves! And each emperor owned three or four times that number.

One reason that Roman society had so many slaves was that slavery was seen as natural. People viewed it as a simple fact of life and believed the gods themselves accepted it. Even most slaves felt this way. Indeed, many slaves who gained their freedom soon purchased their own slaves. The slave owner Isidorus, mentioned above, was a former slave himself!

The dream of freedom

Many Roman slaves hoped to better their social position in life. The only way slaves could do so was to gain their freedom. A few tried escaping or employing violence, but this approach always failed. The Roman army eventually crushed all slave revolts.

This modern drawing shows Roman slaves tending to furnaces that were used to heat Rome's larger homes and public buildings.

There was another path to freedom, however. It was **manumission**, being freed by one's owner. A slave thereby became a **freedman**, or former slave. A few slaves became free as a gesture of thanks from a kind owner for years of loyal service. Or genuine feelings of love might lead to manumission. Also, some slaves managed to buy their freedom. Most household slaves received little gifts of money, like tips, for constant hard work and loyalty. They could spend the money any way they liked. If their masters were willing to allow it, that included saving up to buy their freedom.

In the Roman countryside, many slaves worked on farms, where they helped with planting, harvesting, feeding animals and cleaning barns and stables.

Only a small number of Roman slaves were able to gain their freedom in these ways. Some slaves did not earn tips for their labours. Others did not earn enough, and still others had masters unwilling to free them for any reason. Yet that minority who did gain freedom affected how Roman society operated. Former slaves often took jobs that freeborn Romans did not want. Also, some freedmen were talented and hardworking. They did well in a wide range of jobs.

THE FAILED SLAVE REBELLIONS

Three large-scale slave revolts took place before Augustus established the Empire. The last and most famous was the rebellion of Spartacus, between 73 and 71 BC. While training at a gladiator school, Spartacus escaped along with some others. They freed other slaves and trained them to fight. Spartacus defeated several small Roman armies. But the government finally sent a large one, which crushed the slaves. After that, there were no more Roman slave revolts.

A legend claimed that just before Spartacus's last battle, he killed his horse. He said that if he won he could have any horse in Rome.

The Romans' most common form of relaxation was going to the public baths. In Rome's early centuries, most people did not bathe very often. And when they did, they washed in a river or stream.

Bathhouses

Roman bathing habits changed over time, however, mainly due to the influence of Greek culture. The Greeks had public bathhouses, and by the time Augustus died in AD 14, bathhouses could be found across the Roman lands. The city of Rome alone then had more than 170 of them. The reason so many bathhouses were needed is that almost everyone – men, women, rich and poor – used them on a regular basis. In fact, most people went at least a few times a week.

BATHS OF CARACALLA.

This 19th century painting of the Baths of Caracalla, in Rome, captures the place's incredible size and grandeur.

This gap in the floor of a Roman building reveals part of the system used for heating bathhouses and other structures.

Thermae

The first Roman bathhouses were small. But during the Empire, the government built several enormous ones. Called *thermae*, they could hold thousands of bathers at the same time. Each of the *thermae* had a number of rooms containing pools in which people lounged and washed. Some pools were hot, others cold. And the custom was to go from cold to hot or vice versa.

However, the larger bathhouses were not simply places to get clean. They also had exercise rooms and ball courts to help people keep fit. In addition, there were reading rooms, hair salons and snack bars. And many people simply went to the baths to meet friends.

MEN AND WOMEN BATHERS

Most Romans viewed it as improper for men and women to bathe together in public. So some bathhouses offered separate rooms for women. In others, men and women bathed at different times of the day.

The public games

Most Romans felt that nothing could beat the public games. Firstly, they were huge in scale and exciting. Secondly, admission was free.

Attended by people from all walks of life, the games were held in two main settings. One was an **amphitheatre**, a large oval-shaped stadium. The largest amphitheatre in Rome was the famous Colosseum. It held roughly 50,000 spectators.

The amphitheatre games featured fights between people and animals. There were also trained animal acts. But the highlight of these games was armed combat among gladiators. Trained to fight to the death, they were mostly slaves. But a few free Romans became gladiators to gain fame or experience the thrill of danger. If one fighter wounded or gained control of his opponent, a decision had to be made. Would the downed man live or die? The leading official present sometimes allowed the spectators to help make that decision. Through shouted words and various hand signals, they called for the beaten gladiator to be spared or killed.

A scene from the 1954 film *Demetrius and the Gladiators* shows a group of gladiators saluting the emperor Caligula on the platform in the distance.

This famous painting from 1882 captures the excitement of the contests held in the Circus Maximus.

The circus

The other major games venue was the circus, a massive and very long racetrack. The Empire's biggest was the Circus Maximus in Rome. It was 610 metres (2,000 feet) long and 213 metres (700 feet) wide. There, some 250,000 spectators watched chariot races. The most common chariot was drawn by four horses. The most successful charioteer on record was Pompeius Muscosus, with 3,559 victories!

MANY TYPES OF GLADIATORS

There were many different gladiator types. One had little armour and fought with a net and trident, a long three-pronged spear. Another wore heavy armour and brandished a sword and shield. Still other kinds of gladiators fought with two swords, on horseback or in moving chariots. There were even fighters who clashed while wearing helmets with no eye-holes! They had to search for each other using only sounds and touching. Female gladiators sometimes fought, too.

The Romans were a deeply religious people who worshipped many gods. The relationship between a person and the gods was a sort of bargain. People carried out the traditional sacred **rituals**. In return, the gods showed those worshippers favour. But if a person failed to do his religious duty, the gods might punish him.

People often worshipped daily at home at small shrines. These existed in the atrium or courtyard in larger homes and in almost any room in a poorer house. Many people also attended public ceremonies that took place on religious holidays. These rituals were carried out by official Roman priests.

This bronze figurine of Jupiter, the leader of the Roman gods, once held a thunderbolt in its raised hand and a sceptre in the other.

The Roman Pantheon

Several gods belonged to Rome's official religion. These gods made up the state **pantheon**, meaning a group of gods. They were the traditional gods worshipped since Rome's founding. The leader of the state gods was Jupiter. His divine wife, Juno, protected women and childbirth. Mars was god of war. Neptune ruled the seas, and Venus was goddess of love. Also, Jupiter's handsome young messenger, Mercury, protected travellers and tradesmen.

The Romans were extremely tolerant, which meant they showed great respect for other peoples' gods. And Rome sometimes adopted foreign gods and their rituals. One example was Cybele, a goddess who originated in what is now Turkey. Another was Isis, from Egypt. Still another, Mithras, came from Persia (now Iran).

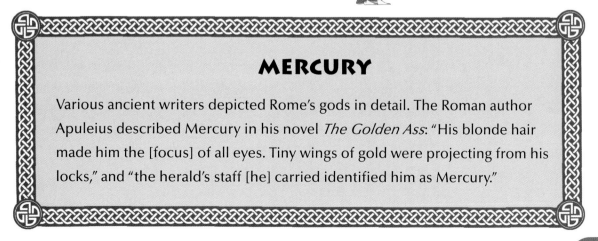

Isis, shown in this ancient painting, was originally an Egyptian mother goddess with magical powers. The Romans adopted her as their own.

MERCURY

Various ancient writers depicted Rome's gods in detail. The Roman author Apuleius described Mercury in his novel *The Golden Ass*: "His blonde hair made him the [focus] of all eyes. Tiny wings of gold were projecting from his locks," and "the herald's staff [he] carried identified him as Mercury."

Common rituals of worship

The most common Roman religious rituals were prayer and **sacrifice**. People of all ages and walks of life prayed often. Sometimes they prayed informally, at home or almost anywhere. The Romans prayed for many of the things modern people do.

It was also common to pray in a more formal way. Formal prayer usually happened before a shrine – either private or public – on a religious holiday. During such a holiday, people had the day off work. Many took part in a public religious festival. There were about a dozen major ones and several minor ones each year.

Other common customs enacted during religious festivals included feasting, marching in parades intended to honour the gods, and doing traditional dances.

This Roman altar, dedicated to the gods Mars and Venus, was created during the reign of the emperor Trajan (AD 98-117).

Priests led an animal to be sacrificed to an altar. They cut its throat and sliced up its body. Finally, they tossed some of the parts into a sacred fire. People believed that the gods happily breathed in the rising smoke.

Sacred sacrifices

The second major religious ritual, sacrifice, took place during all religious festivals and ceremonies. Sacrifices were offerings made to satisfy the gods. Particularly common was sacrificing items meant to feed the gods. These included plants, wine, honey and the bodies of animals. Sheep, goats and cows were the most common kinds. Anyone could make such offerings privately, for instance on a farm or at a shrine in a city home. But public sacrifices were carried out by priests at altars located near the public temples. People of all social classes gathered nearby to watch as the priest sacrificed an animal.

PARILIA

An important spring festival was the Parilia, held on 21 April. A celebration of Rome's founding, it involved several colourful customs. Farmers cleaned their sheep pens and decorated them with green plants. Then they lit bonfires. Gathering their sheep, they led the animals through the smoke to make them pure in the gods' eyes.

The Christians triumph

During the early Empire, a new religion emerged. Called Christianity, it began in Roman-controlled Palestine (now Israel). It was based on the teachings of the Jewish preacher Jesus. He was executed in Jerusalem in about AD 30–33. At first, his followers continued to call themselves Jews. But by about AD 50 or so they had broken away from **Judaism**.

At first, other Romans viewed the Christians as troublemakers or criminals. And many Christians suffered **persecution**. Some were harassed. Others were beaten or even killed. This hatred for Christians had nothing to do with which god they worshipped. Instead, it was based partly on faulty information about them. False rumours spread that they killed and ate babies during their rituals. Mistrust of Christians also came from their refusal to worship the emperor along with their god. All other Roman religions followed that custom.

NERO'S PERSECUTION

The first major persecution of Christians occurred in AD 64. That year a terrible fire devastated Rome. Some people suspected that Emperor Nero started the fire. That rumour was probably false. But Nero sought to divert attention from himself so he blamed the Christians. The Roman historian Tacitus witnessed the horrifying persecution. Many Christians, he wrote, "were torn to pieces by dogs, or crucified, or made into torches to be ignited after dark".

But despite the mistreatment they suffered, the Christians bravely maintained their beliefs. They met and worshipped in secret when necessary.

This situation changed in the early AD 300s. The emperor Constantine came to see the Christians and their god as allies. So he ordered that Christians be accepted and treated like everyone else. By the late 300s, Christianity was the Empire's official religion.

The cruel emperor Nero watches as the Christians he has condemned are tortured.

Modern civilization owes a tremendous debt to the ancient Romans. People often say the Roman Empire "fell" in AD 476. Yet it was mainly its government that ceased to exist. Many Roman ideas, beliefs and customs survived.

The rituals of worship used by these modern Italian Christians developed largely during the Roman Empire's last two centuries.

Rome's religion is a good example. When the Empire crumbled, Christianity was its official religion. It continued to be so for medieval Europe. As the centuries wore on, Christianity spread across the globe. Today, it is the world's largest religion.

The Romans' main language, Latin, is another example. Over time, it steadily changed into several other languages, such as French, Spanish and Italian. Moreover, Latin's original version remains the Roman Catholic Church's official language.

Still another aspect of Roman culture that still exists today is Rome's system of laws. It became the basis for most modern legal systems.

ROMAN WATCHMEN

Many modern professions are based directly on ancient Roman ones. The widely admired occupation of the firefighter is only one. Today's firefighters are quite similar to the "Watchmen". They were professional firefighters introduced by Rome's first emperor, Augustus. He knew that numerous fires ravaged the Roman capital almost every year. But there was no one trained to fight them. So he created a team of slaves specially trained to do that job. The next time you drive by your local fire station, remember that Augustus, a Roman, made its existence possible.

A day in the life of a child in Ancient Rome

My name is Avita and I am twelve years old. I live near Rome with my mother, father, and two younger brothers. We have a large villa. My father is a merchant and we live a comfortable life.

After I awake I get dressed into my tunic and tie a belt at my waist.

Slaves prepare our breakfast and I help to serve the bread and fruit, then I eat with my brothers. My brothers go to school. I don't go to school and it can get lonely in the day. Mother says I must learn how to run a household. Father already has a husband in mind for me and says I must prepare for marriage.

My mother leaves for the baths, while I stay behind and do some weaving. I am helping my mother weave a new toga for father. My mother is very skilled at weaving. I hope I will get as good as her before I marry.

We have a light lunch and then my brothers come home and we all have a siesta. The sun is hot and it's so nice to lie down in a cool room for a while. After our sleep, the boys go back to school.

My tutor visits for a short time in the afternoon. I am learning to read and write. The house is busy today because my father is entertaining guests this evening. He is keen to impress them and the cook is preparing amazing food such as wild boar and peacock. Everyone is rushing about, arranging couches and tables and carrying huge silver platters and jugs of wine. I peek in the dining room – the mosaics and paintings look beautiful – the guests are sure to be impressed.

My brothers and I have bread and meat for dinner, followed by ice cream for a treat. We will be expected to keep out of the way once the guests arrive. We play with our pet dog until the sun goes down then creep off to bed.

43

753 BC
According to tradition, Rome is founded by the twins Romulus and Remus

AROUND 600 BC
Earliest evidence of Latin writing

500 BC
Temples are built

509 BC
The Roman Republic is founded

450 BC
First Roman law codes are made

329 BC
The Circus Maximus is built in Rome. It is rebuilt and expanded over several centuries

312 BC
The Appian Way (an important Roman road) and the first Roman aqueduct, the Aqua Appia, are built

AROUND 280 BC
Earliest evidence of Roman coins

272 BC
Rome wins control of all of Italy

264 BC
First gladiatorial games are held

206 BC
Spain becomes two Roman provinces

146 BC
North Africa becomes a Roman province

AROUND 100 BC
A businessman called Gaius Sergius Orata invents the hypocaust heating system

63 BC
Octavian, who will later become Rome's first emperor, is born

46 BC
Julius Caesar becomes the first dictator of Rome. He introduces the Julian calendar

44 BC
Julius Caesar is assassinated

27 BC

Octavian becomes Augustus, the first Roman emperor. This marks the beginning of the Roman Empire

AD 14

Emperor Augustus dies

AD 43

Rome conquers Britain

AROUND AD 50

The Romans begin to use transparent glass for the windows of their homes

AD 64

A major fire breaks out and devastates much of Rome. The emperor Nero blames the Christians and persecution of Christians begins.

AD 70-80

The Colosseum is built in Rome

AD 79

Mount Vesuvius, a volcano overlooking the Bay of Naples in western Italy, erupts violently. Nearby towns, including Pompeii, are buried under ash and debris.

AD 118-125

The Emperor Hadrian builds the Pantheon

AD 212

Roman citizenship is given to all free people in the Roman Empire

AD 306

Constantine becomes the first Christian emperor

AD 476

The last Roman emperor, Romulus Augustus, is defeated by Odoacer, a Gothic general. Rome's government ceases to exist.

AD stands for *anno domini* - after the birth of Jesus Christ

amphitheatre large, oval-shaped stadium in which the Romans staged public games, including those in which gladiators fought

atrium well-decorated entrance hall of an upper-class Roman house

BC before the birth of Jesus Christ

civil war war between two sides from within the same country

client in the patronage system, a lower-class person who did favours for an upper-class one

engineer professional builder with knowledge of building materials and methods

freedman former slave (a term used today to describe both male and female freed slaves)

hypocaust heating device in which hot air from a fire moved into an open space beneath a building

Judaism religion of the Jews, from which Christianity grew

manumission process of freeing a slave

midwife woman trained to deliver other women's babies

mosaic artistic image or scene made up of hundreds or thousands of tiny tiles, stones, shells or other materials

pantheon group of gods worshipped by a nation or people. The Pantheon is a large circular building in Rome dedicated to the gods.

papyrus water plant from Egypt. In ancient times, paper was made from papyrus.

paterfamilias father or other male family head in a Roman home

patron in the patronage system, an upper-class person who helped one or more clients in exchange for various favours

patronage Roman social system in which one person did favours for a wealthier person in exchange for financial or other kinds of help

persecution act of unfairly attacking someone for their beliefs, customs, race or gender

republic country where the people who make the laws and run the government are chosen by the people

rhetoric art of public speaking or persuasive speech

ritual set way of going through the steps of a religious ceremony

sacrifice offering made to appease a god or gods

sewer underground pipe that carries waste away

shrine special place built in memory of a person or to honour a god

social status how important a person is seen as being in a society

tenement large block of flats in a city

villa comfortable country house

Books

Ancient Rome (Eyewitness), Simon James (Dorling Kindersley, 2011)

Ancient Rome (Navigators), Philip Steele (Kingfisher, 2012)

Roman Britain (History on Your Doorstep), Alex Woolf (Franklin Watts, 2012)

Romans (Weird True Facts), Moira Butterfield (Franklin Watts, 2014)

Websites

www.bbc.co.uk/schools/primaryhistory/romans

This BBC website has lots of information about the Romans.

www.britishmuseum.org/explore/young_explorers/discover/all_about/roman_treasure.aspx

Find out all about Roman treasure on the British Museum's website.

www.educationscotland.gov.uk/scotlandshistory/caledonianspictsromans/romansinscotland

Learn more about the Romans on the Education Scotland site.

DVDs

Demetrius and the Gladiators (20th Century Fox, 1954; released on DVD in 2013)

In the Shadow of Vesuvius (National Geographic, 2010)

Rome: Engineering an Empire (A+E Home Video, 2007)

Places to visit

The British Museum, London

www.britishmuseum.org

At the British Museum, you can see and find out about many Roman objects.

National Roman Legion Museum, Wales

www.museumwales.ac.uk/roman

Discover how the Romans lived at Caerleon in Wales.

How can I find out more?

One of the most entertaining ways to find out more about ancient Rome is to watch films about the Romans and then do research to find out what was accurate in those films and what was inaccurate.